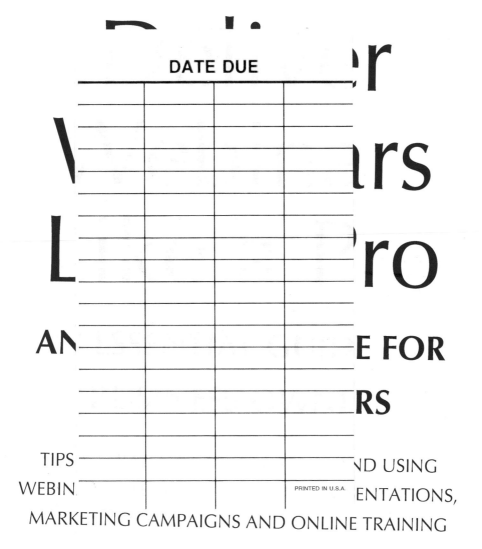

DATE DUE

PRINTED IN U.S.A.

r

rs

ro

AN E FOR

RS

TIPS ND USING
WEBIN ENTATIONS,
MARKETING CAMPAIGNS AND ONLINE TRAINING

Melodie Rush & Carl Stearns
#1 Bestselling A

Table of Contents

Meet the Authors

Melodie Rush is an experienced speaker and webinar presenter, having led more than 1000 webinars since 2001, and attended at least four times that many. In that time, she has seen it all, from great webinars that drove results to those where time slowed to a crawl as the presenter droned on. She has presented to many fortune 500 companies with webinar audiences of 1 attendee to several 100. Melodie knows what works and what doesn't. Melodie lives in Erie, CO and loves traveling, volunteering at the zoo and taking photos.

Please connect:

- Website www.melodierush.com
- FaceBook - www.facebook.com/wecreatemvps
- Twitter https://twitter.com/WeCreateMVPs
- LinkedIn - https://www.linkedin.com/in/melodierush
- GooglePlus - https://plus.google.com/+MelodieRush1
- Find my Podcast on iTunes, Stitcher and Google Play: The Webinar Report

Carl Stearns is a digital marketing technology consultant and speaker that has been using online meeting and webinar technology for sales, software support and live online education/training since 2000. Currently, Carl works with A/E professionals, businesses, consultants, doctors, government agencies and manufacturers helping to leverage online technology to directly affect lead generation and sales of their products and services. Carl lives in the resort town of Coeur d'Alene, Idaho where he enjoys boating, wake-boarding and skiing.

Please connect:

- Website www.civicmindmedia.com
- FaceBook - www.facebook.com/carlstearns
- Twitter https://twitter.com/carlstearns
- LinkedIn - https://www.linkedin.com/in/civicmindmedia/
- GooglePlus - https://plus.google.com/+CarlStearns-Marketing-Consultant

Introduction

Welcome to Deliver Webinars Like a Pro. This book is an Essential Guide for Business Owners and represents more than 15 years of experience from both Melodie and Carl.

We are so excited to share our knowledge with you and are happy to help you on your journey to delivering high quality online presentations. In this book we discuss the planning, setting up and executing of webinars for both the corporate world and small businesses. You will learn how webinars can be used for sales presentations, marketing campaigns, online training and customer support. We address technology requirements, paid and free services, as well has how to make money with webinars.

Please share with us any questions you may have. Also if you find mistakes in this book please let us know by contacting us using the information on The Author page right before the this introduction and table of contents.

We look forward to hearing about your success with webinars.

Additional Resources

To get a list of resources, join our Facebook Group, and get updates to this book go to
www.DeliverWebinars.com

Chapter One

An Introduction to Webinars

What is a webinar?

The term webinar is a simple play on words, combining the word web with seminar. Simply put, a webinar is a seminar which is transmitted through the internet to participants using video, slideshow, screenshare, and audio conferencing software and services.

Webinars typically involve a presenter, a producer and attendees (often referred to as the audience). Participants can view anything, from a live video stream to documents or applications currently being used in real time on the presenter's computer screen.

Participants in a webinar are provided with login information and, in most cases, use a web browser to engage in the conference. The primary benefit of a webinar is that people can attend from any location in the world - as long as they have access to the internet.

There are many types of online conferencing; below you will find a description of several of the more common terms.

Webcast

Basically, a webcast is what it sounds like: it's the internet counterpart to a traditional radio or TV broadcast; a broadcast or live streaming over the web. In this kind of situation, you could think of it like watching TV. You are not really interacting with the presenter; you are watching something over the web. Webcasts, though similar to webinars, do not allow the audience to ask questions or take polls during the presentation.

Web conference

A web conference is more like a team meeting of members of a group that meets regularly, with the singular difference that you get together and interact over the web instead of in person. Being in a web conference is like being in a traditional conference room, except you are meeting with your team online. There is often a lot of interaction and it is typically a smaller group than a webcast or a webinar. A moderator manages the web conference by passing audio and presentation control among participants.

Web meeting

Much like a web conference, a web meeting is usually a small group of people who all have the ability to speak with each other through the live streaming audio/video, by sharing desktops all at once. Since everyone has the ability to speak during the meeting it is necessary to keep the group to a minimum (often 10 or less).

Webinar

A webinar was originally like attending an educational lecture over the web; much like a traditional lecture, participants can "raise their hands" to ask questions of the presenter. Webinars may involve more than one presenter; however, the majority of people participating in a webinar are listening to the webinar, in much the same way you might in a college classroom containing 200 students. Webinars allow for interaction between the participant and the presenter.

Today, people often use these terms interchangeably. Webinar is now the generic term for any type of live streaming meeting over the web.

Benefits of a Webinar

The two main benefits of offering a webinar are:

Eliminates Travel

1. Webinars are an efficient way to transmit and share information.
2. A webinar allows you to interact with many people in many different locations.
3. As a presenter, you can use webinars to demonstrate software or present your product or service to clients - without ever leaving your office.

Saves Time

1. Eliminating travel not only cuts costs, it also saves you time.
2. Conducting and attending webinars, rather than off-location in-person meetings and seminars, means spending more of your time in the training, where it counts, rather than in travel.
3. Webinars give you and your staff more opportunities to learn, grow and sell with minimal interruption to your workday.

Webinars allow you to do a lot of things

You can teach, share information, provide product support, demonstrate a service, sell a product or control a participating computer. It's also possible to generate revenue conducting a webinar. Webinars can be used to convert leads to sales, deliver business training programs for a fee, tutor students, conduct online based college courses... and the list goes on. Record the webinar, and now you have an online training program that can be delivered as an on-demand webcast over and over again.

Here's a good example of how the use of webinar technology has increased business opportunity while saving time and money: one of our clients is a group of retired veterinarians who developed a program to train veterinary technicians. The vet tech training includes everything from the metric system and basic chemistry to surgical procedures and emergency medicine. Just a couple years ago, the classroom-based course was taught at several different locations throughout the state by a variety of staff instructors.

Through webinar and online training technology, we transformed the business so that the course is taught entirely online. Travel was completely eliminated for the instructors, as well as for the students. Classroom locations were no longer necessary, so classroom lease fees were eliminated and the number of paid staff instructors was reduced. Enrollments have tripled; the business is highly profitable. Most importantly, due to the live streaming nature of the program, students remain engaged and on task. And best of all: successful student completion of the program is over 98%. This no small feat when you consider the program is conducted live, four hours each night, four days a week, over the course of seventeen weeks. Our clients couldn't be happier.

Join Our Facebook Group

Go to www.DeliverWebinars.com

Chapter Two

What You Need to Conduct a Webinar

Equipment, Software and Services

Amazingly, there really isn't a lot of equipment necessary to conduct a webinar. In fact, most modern laptop and desktop computers (event some Smartphones) come with the minimum necessary equipment already built-in. This chapter will break down the discussion into three categories: hardware, software and services.

Hardware

For hardware, you need a computer that is preferably connected to a high-speed internet service, wired not wireless is preferred. A microphone may also be necessary, if you plan to use the webinar services VoIP (Voice over Internet Protocol; or, basically, streaming live audio over the internet) or you decide to use a telephone conferencing solution. In some cases you can use both; we will discuss these in more detail later, under the "Services" section.

In the corporate world, telephones are still used in delivering the audio portion of most webinars. For smaller companies or individuals, usually a microphone connected to the computer is used in the majority of the webinars. Melodie uses a Yeti brand microphone - but there are certainly lots of choices on the market. In fact, the microphone on your laptop may be sufficient. It's always best to test before you do a webinar to check the quality of the audio.

For live video streaming webinars like video conferencing, you will need a webcam. Once again, the webcam on your laptop computer may be sufficient for webinar purposes. If you're using a desktop computer or laptop computer without a built-in webcam, you can purchase one separately for about $50-$100. And just like the microphone test the quality of your video from your webcam before engaging in webinars.

An optional piece of hardware you should consider is a second monitor. This is one of those things that seems like an unnecessary luxury reserved for true geeks; however, we promise you that once you start using a second (or third) monitor, you won't understand how you ever lived without it. Though practical for just about all computer uses, here are some of the benefits a second monitor offers you when conducting webinars:

When conducting a webinar by yourself (that is, you are producing it by yourself - hopefully not attending it alone!), then a second monitor offers a perfect place to display your notes. To accomplish this, set up the webinar service to only show one monitor to your audience and hide the other monitor. This means that you can bring up your notes or queue websites or software applications you want to display in your presentation and perhaps even display the list of participants. If you use PowerPoint or Keynote, you can use the second monitor to display a preview and time, as well as the next slide.

A second monitor is indeed handy. It's so much more productive to have multiple monitors; and if you use them once, you will probably never go back to a single monitor again. Carl uses three - and if he could justify the expense, I'm sure he would use six.

Software

Once again, it doesn't take much software to conduct a webinar. In fact, most of the software you need is already on your computer, or is optional. Here's a rundown of the minimum necessary software:

Operating system

Sure, this one is obvious; but the reason we brought it up is to point out that the minimum software necessary to conduct a webinar is already on your computer. Operating systems such as Windows and Mac offer installed or add-on basic software to take screenshots, present slides on a screen and record video. No, we didn't forget Linux. However, if you're using Linux as your operating system, your skills are probably already beyond the context of this book.

Slide presentation software

During your webinar you may want to present slides with information, just like you would during an in-person seminar. The most popular slide presentation software is Microsoft PowerPoint. If you already have Microsoft Office, great; you're all set to go. Mac users have another option in Keynote; a third option is Google Slides; a fourth option is Open Office Impress. Impress is a free open-source slide creation and presentation software that you can download from here: http://www.openoffice.org/product/

Internet browser

You absolutely will need a browser on your computer to access the webinar service (discussed in the next section). Your operating system most likely already came with a browser, be it

Internet Explorer or Safari. Both Melodie and Carl recommend that you install multiple browsers on your computer, so that you have a backup if you need it. Sometimes, just prior to a webinar, we find that our preferred browser is not operating properly, due to a setting or recent updates to the browser. Rather than panicking last minute and trying to find the correct setting, we will try one of our alternative browsers. If that works, great; we move on. If not, well, then it's time to calm down and find that pesky setting. You should have on your computer at least three browsers: any three of Internet Explorer or Safari or Firefox or Chrome. One of these will become your go-to favorite.

- Internet Explorer - http://www.microsoft.com/en-us/download/internet-explorer.aspx
- Safari - http://support.apple.com/downloads/#safari
- Firefox – http://GetFirefox.com
- Chrome - https://www.google.com/intl/en/chrome/browser/

Screen Capture Software (optional)

Screen capture software is a great tool to enable you to take screenshots which you can include in your presentation - or to take screenshots of your presentation for later use. Both Windows and Mac come with basic screen capture capabilities. There are many solutions you can purchase or download for free on the internet, which include additional capabilities such as editing and adding elements to your captured images.

1. **SnagIt**. This is a paid software which works very well and has a full assortment of features you may find useful beyond webinars. Melodie uses this program exclusively. Mac, Windows and Linux versions. http://www.techsmith.com/snagit.html

2. **Quick Screenshot Maker.** Includes a free and a paid version. Carl has been using this program for years. Windows. http://www.etrusoft.com/screenshot-maker/

3. **Screengrab!** This program works through an add-on to the Mozilla Firefox browser. The primary benefit of this program is that it will let you capture an entire browser page rather than only what is displayed on the screen. Carl has been using this for years. https://addons.mozilla.org/en-US/firefox/addon/screengrab-fix-version/

Recording Software (optional)

Getting a recording of your presentation for later use is a major advantage of conducting webinars. For example, you can set the recorded webinar up for replay, use it in training program or include them in your informational products; we'll talk more about that later in the book. Most webinar services include a recording feature - you just need to remember to turn it on.

Frankly, this is the best way to record the webinar in cases where you have more than one presenter in different locations and you're using live video streaming. The resulting video and audio will be in sync. However, it is nice to have a backup program, such as ScreenFlow (Mac) or Camtasia (Windows or Mac) on your computer to record the webinar.

Mind mapping software

If you're looking for a way to organize your thoughts for your presentation, then mind mapping software could be a great help; Carl uses FreeMind

https://www.google.com/intl/en/chrome/browser/

Many people also display the resulting mind map on a slide during the presentation as a guide and/or offer it as a download too. We have also seen people do entire presentations using mind mapping software as their visuals.

Webinar services

The most important service you will need is the webinar service itself. There are many companies that offer webinar and internet conferencing services. Most of these are offered as paid services, where you pay a monthly fee to use it; some do, however, offer free services. There are probably well over 50 different services on the market today. We divided them into the following five categories:

1. Professional Corporate Services

Melodie uses services from this category in her corporate job. Professional corporate services include Cisco's WebEx and Event Center, Adobe Connect Pro and Microsoft Live Meetings. These are the professional ones which the big companies will have and they include many nice-to-have features built in to them. Frankly, many of the services in the next category, Commercial services, also now include these same features.

2. Commercial Services

Commercial services include Cisco's GoToMeeting and GoToWebinar, Zoom, ReadyTalk, MeetingBurner, JoinMe, FuzeBox, BrightTALK, MeetCheap, Webinars On Air and Webinar Express... and there are many, many, many more. Almost all of these provide a 30-day free trial. We encourage you to try out a few and find the one that works for you; both Carl and Melodie use GoToWebinar, Zoom and JoinMe on a frequent basis.

3. Free Services

There are also free services: AnyMeeting, MeetingBurner, Google Hangouts and Zoom. If you are just getting started out and you have fairly small audiences, you can use AnyMeeting, which allows up to 200 people in attendance. The free service is supported by advertising, so you will need to consider whether or not you want such advertising displayed during your webinars. MeetingBurner will allow you to have up to ten attendees for free. Zoom also has a free option. It allows sessions for up to 50 attendees for 40 minutes or less. And the newest free player on the block is Google Hangouts, which has many nice features - but at this point, is new and not as established as the others.

4. Automated Services

These are services where you can record your webinar, upload it to the service provider and let it run in an automated fashion. Automated services include EverWebinar and TPNI Engage.

5. Hybrid Services

There are a few hybrid services that offer automation as well as live webinars. WebinarJam Studio, Easy Webinar, Google Hangouts Plugin and Stealth Seminar are the most popular.

We are often asked, "Which is the best webinar service to use?" and the answer is to look at essential features. If you are just starting out or don't like to deal with too much tech, you want a service that is not only reliable but very easy to use and has online tech support. We guarantee that if you do many webinars, you are going to need some type of support. All of the services have improved in the last few years; however, be aware that there are still issues once in a while, so it's nice to have someplace to go to get help.

Today, people expect to be able to listen to the webinar over their computers, so you want to make sure that the service you have includes audio streaming. I also think it's important if the service you use allows people to watch the webinar on their tablet or smartphone. A significant number of people today use a tablet or smartphone instead of their computer to watch webinars - you don't want to lock them out.

If you have more than one presenter, you will want a feature that allows you to switch back and forth among presenters. This feature allows you to pass over presenter controls of the slides, the audio and the video to others on the call.

All of these webinar services have some features in common and some differentiating features. Once you have determined the features, you will need take a look at the cost of the webinar service, which has those features.

Deliver Webinars Like A Pro

Recommended service

One of the most important features you will need to have is the ability to register attendees. Most of the services discussed above have this feature built-in. However, Melodie and Carl also offer a software service which not only registers attendees, but also reminds them of the upcoming webinar using email, text and voicemail. Also, this software automatically follows up with the people who attended the webinar and sends a separate automated follow-up to those who did not attend. Though optional, these features are very important to marketers looking to use webinars to increase conversions based on webinar attendance.

Cost of Conducting Webinars

"What is the typical cost for conducting a webinar?" is a question that implies there are costs beyond the cost of the webinar service itself.

First, the cost depends on the webinar service that you choose. Some of the services are much more expensive because they have more tools or features, as well as a proven track record. Most webinar services are priced on the maximum number of people it will allow to attend at once. Payment plans are either monthly or annual. There are free services such as Google Hangouts and a few others out there, but they don't have the rich set of features as the paid services - so that's the trade-off.

However, if you're a real marketing tech geek, like Carl, you'd love be an early adopter of these new services.

Other costs that you might choose to incur would be to hire a producer to help you promote, produce and deliver the webinar. You may also use paid marketing to attract prospects to attend the webinar.

Think of creating a webinar in terms of marketing, so you are either saving money or making money. In this case, your webinar really shouldn't cost a dime at the end of the day. Just gain enough leads from the webinar to deliver to your sales staff to help you more than pay for the webinar in more product or service sales. In terms of using a webinar to save money, simply add up what it might have cost to have an in-person seminar, including hotel, travel, food, etc. - and a webinar at just about any cost will look inexpensive and allow you to meet with your remote team on a frequent basis.

Think in terms of opportunity, rather than expense; but of course, you always need start-up funds to get things going. There's always ways to make money or save money with webinars.

Don't let cost determine whether or not you get started using webinars in your business. If it makes sense for you in your business or in your personal life to start doing webinars, there are free services available. You can get started - and then move

Deliver Webinars Like A Pro

on to the other services should you need them. For example, Google Hangouts, the new kid on the block, has more features than any service that was in existence two years ago. All of the services add more features with each release.

Get A Recommended List Of Resources

To get a recommended list of resources (updated often with new services) go to www.DeliverWebinars.com

Chapter Three

Styles, Formats, and Timing

Webinars can be delivered in many different styles, including presentations, lectures, software demonstrations, tutorials, workshops and interviews, as well as discussions or interactive meetings. The three most commonly used styles are: Interview, Lecture and Screen Sharing.

Interview style

Of all methods we have used, this one is the easiest and often the default style used by both of us. The interview style requires at least two people as presenters in the webinar. The two presenters can be remotely located from each other, which works very well; but quite frankly, having both people in the same room does make interaction easier and more natural. In this style of webinar, one person acts as the host and the other as the expert. Often, the host is also an expert who provides valuable information during the webinar; but the host's primary job is to maintain the flow of the webinar and keep it on track.

Lecture style

This is probably the most common style used today because it only requires one presenter. The lecture style is also one of the most familiar, since it is a basic unit of our education growing up and used today commonly in online education.

Using a lecture style, one presenter presents the information using streaming audio and either a live video stream and/or a slide deck. These work best when trying to convey a specific educational point or when demonstrating a product or software. This style is easy to do and requires little in way of coordination, but does require the presenter to have a practiced presentation, since he or she will not have a second party helping to keep the discussion flowing.

Screen sharing

Another common and very popular webinar style is screen sharing. In fact, screen sharing webinars were the very first webinars both of us started conducting in our careers. Screen sharing webinars can be used on a one-to-one or one-to-many basis, making it easy to demonstrate software applications, provide technical support and/or deliver online training. Depending upon the webinar service used, the presenter can request control of a participant's computer. In this way, they can show how something is done directly on their computer, while others learn by watching. Screen sharing is perfect for supporting customers and has proven to be an incredible tool to the sales and marketing teams of many companies around the world.

Recommended Length of a Webinar

A good rule of thumb for a webinar (in fact, for any type of presentation) is to be long enough to cover the topic - and no longer. That might seem like a cop-out answer to this commonly-asked question, but it is absolutely true. Think of any presentation you've attended that you felt went on too long; in most cases, it was due to the presenter not practicing and not editing the presentation enough. Many of these long presentations occur when the presenter presents the information off the top of his or her head and ends up going on several tangents. So, like we said in the beginning, your presentation should be long enough to cover the topic and not a second longer.

Now on the other hand, it has also been long understood that people don't usually stay engaged in a presentation for much more than two hours at most. This applies to both in-person and online presentations. Online presentations have additional considerations, in that participants are in a familiar setting with many distractions that could easily remove them from your webinar. Therefore, we recommend that you practice, then edit, then practice, then edit, then practice (you get the point) your webinar until you can thoroughly cover your top in no more than 60 to 90 minutes. Approximately, 90% of all webinars run around 60 minutes.

A 60-minute webinar is typically structured with 45 to 50 minutes of content, leaving 10 to 15 minutes for a question-and-answer period. If your audience is large and highly-engaged (i.e. asking questions), you could easily extend a webinar to 90 minutes. Anything over 90 minutes and you must provide a break - for obvious reasons.

We recommend that you experiment with the length of your webinar presentations. For example, one of our clients was interested in reaching the executive level employees in corporations nationwide with a sales presentation webinar. Before working with us, his webinars ran from 60 to 90 minutes each; but most attendees were lower and middle management level, rather than the top decision-makers where his conversion rates were the highest. Recognizing that schedules of most executives are full of meetings, we started promoting 20-minute webinars that would cover one single topic of interest; this doubled the overall sign-up and show-up rate of executives.

Days and Times of Day for Conducting Webinars

The problem with most rules of thumb is that they don't often consider a specific audience, industry, market or culture. The best day and time for a webinar really depends on all of those things. For example, Melodie works with large corporations conducting training and support webinars. So, in her case, she has found best attendance occurs at webinars held at 1:00 PM Eastern Time, which allows employees nationwide to attend during normal work hours. She has also found that Mondays and Fridays are not always the best days to conduct a webinar in the corporate environment. However, there are exceptions to this rule; and we have had success on these days and at other specific times as well.

On the other hand, if you're trying to reach an audience outside of their typical work hours, we have found that Friday night can be a great time for a webinar. If you have an international audience, 2:00 PM Eastern Time has proven to work well on Wednesdays; this has been a good time to attract a combined United States and European audience.

It also depends on what type of webinar you are giving. If it's a sales presentation, you are going to have to be more strategic with your time. If you are doing a presentation in terms of support or an internal corporate training, then you have to look at the culture of the organization and decide whether or not you will get the key stakeholders to the meeting at that time. We have an online training client that breaks all of the "rules": webinars are four hours long, held Monday through Thursday, from 6:00 PM to 10:00 PM, for 17 weeks straight. Attendance is near perfect every night. Of course, the attendees pay quite a bit of money up front for the training, which has proven to be a very good motivator.

We hold a lot of webinars at noon for the local attendees. We call them "Lunch and Learns" and we do them at lunchtime for different companies. This timing tends to be good; the attendees can grab their lunch and watch. For other people, lunchtime might not be a good time.

The desire to determine the best day and time of day to hold a webinar comes from a desire to hold a webinar only once, rather than a desire to reach your audience. We suggest that you open your thinking to repeating your webinars to allow your audience to choose the day and time that is convenient for them. This is especially necessary when using webinars to sell, and even more essential if your audience is located in different time zones throughout the world.

Repeating webinars

There are a number of reasons we might recommend repeating a webinar. The first was mentioned above; repeat a webinar to offer a variety of times and dates for attendance. Another would be to best leverage your content while there is demand for the information.

For example, we conducted a webinar for a client that had a large market in both the US and Australia. We conducted the webinar live at 10:00 am US Mountain Time, and then repeated live again at a time that worked best for people in Australia. You need to know whom your audience is and where they are located; and often, you will find it's good to repeat your webinar to meet the demand.

Experiment with days and times of day for your audience. Another option is to schedule your webinar for a couple of times during the same day to determine which time is best or to attract more people overall. We have found that by doing this we often get people that attended the earlier webinar recommending their friends and colleagues to attend the later session. Think of your webinar as a Broadway Show; increase overall attendance by offering a variety of times and days to attend. A bonus to this strategy is that you will get better and better as you present it. You can certainly record the webinar and use the recording for subsequent webinars - we will discuss the pros and cons of this strategy later in the book.

Addressing the second point, leveraging content; it is critical that you leverage the effort you have made to create and deliver a webinar, especially if you follow our advice of practice – edit

– practice – edit – practice. Create a solid presentation; get really good at delivering it and add it to your library of presentations; now schedule that presentation for the entire year. Choose the dates up front when you will deliver that presentation and mark on the calendar the dates you will promote each session. Leveraging your presentation in this manner will make you a polished expert and enable you to get the most from your hard work.

Get The Ultimate Webinar Planning Checklist

To get the Ultimate Webinar Planning Checklist (includes step by step for before, during and after) go to
www.DeliverWebinars.com

Chapter Four

Marketing Your Webinar

Up until now we've covered what a webinar is, the technology required to deliver a webinar and some of the styles and formats that are used to present webinars. Now let's discuss some ways to get people to attend your webinar.

A successful webinar is a webinar that is attended by the intended audience. Many people focus most of their energy on the presentation itself and neglect the matter of promotion as a last-minute item. This is a big mistake; in most cases, it can result in you wasting all of your time creating the presentation. Worse yet, it could kill your confidence in continuing to use webinars.

Certainly, we can't cover every marketing strategy used to promote webinars in this one chapter; there are so many means of promotion that the subject could be covered in several books. What we can do though, is give you some strategies, concepts and best practices that will help you give your inner creative genius a kick-start.

Use your own list

This one probably seems a bit obvious at first, but we often find that our clients are so focused on attracting new customers that they ignore their current customers in the marketing process. Webinars are a great choice to subtly market to your existing customers through tutorials, support sessions and demonstrations. I highly recommend that you start right there and invite people already on your list. At the same time, ask them to recommend your upcoming webinar to their colleagues.

For those of you that are conducting webinars for internal employees of your corporation, marketing is equally important, but the only advantage you have is access to a specific list. You must still promote the webinar; use a headline that captures their attention and get buy-ins to increase attendance rates.

So don't leave marketing as a last step. We recommend that you consider how you're going to promote your webinar before you create the presentation. Doing this will help you define the target audience, their needs and the style of webinar that will work best. It will also give you a schedule, which you can use to make sure that you're not scrambling trying to get the word out with just a day or two before the webinar.

Build a List

Perhaps you don't have an internal or external list available to you. In this case, you need to get started right now on building one. What do we mean when we say "list"? There are probably a thousand meanings for this, but the simplest definition is a list of names and email addresses (and/or additional contact information) of people that have either expressed interest in your services or are currently clients. Today, most lists are composed of email addresses; but don't underestimate the power of direct mail in some cases too.

Building a list is not necessarily as hard as you might think. In fact, you may already have a list. Carl once had an engineering firm as a client. When asked about a customer-marketing list, the client insisted that they had never built an email list of prospective customers and that beyond billing addresses, the firm didn't have anything that could be used. Carl pointed out that the firm had over 75 professional engineers who had interacted with current and prospective customers every day for the last 50 years. Each of those engineers easily had 100+ names and email addresses in their Outlook contacts. So, 75 x 100 was a list of approximately 7,500 names and email addresses; a list. The promotional campaign was then directed at the internal engineers, by giving them the marketing materials and encouraging them to share with their contacts. This resulted in a 50% opt-in rate for the overall campaign - a great start to the building of an "internal list" for marketing the firm.

Webinars which provide helpful and valuable information, which people can use immediately, are perfect candidates for advertising on social media. Facebook, LinkedIn, Twitter, YouTube and online blogs provide a way to put your information right in front of your target market. Just make sure that you offer them something valuable, in order to encourage them to give you their name and email address so that you can build your list for current and future webinars.

Video marketing through YouTube, Facebook, Vimeo and your website is also a great way to build your list. Best of all, your initial and ongoing webinars provide recordings that you can use to create these promotional videos. Use some or all of a past webinar in a video with a message in the lower third or at the end, that states something like this: "If you've found the information in this video helpful, sign up to get advanced notice of upcoming live webinar training sessions at www._____ .com."

Be creative and track your promotions; try different things and test them. That is the best advice we can give in regard to marketing. Don't give up the first time something doesn't work - learn from it and try something else.

Promotion schedule

"When should I start promoting a webinar?" is a common question we get from clients. This comes from the common belief that marketing is the last step in the process. That is a mistake.

As we stated above, start the entire process with marketing in mind; start some sort of soft marketing immediately, if possible. This soft marketing could be polling your list about potential topics, times and interests. For example, you could email your list telling them that your team is putting together a training series on x and that you would like to get opinions on subjects of interest or problems that should be addressed. Not only are you getting some information that will help develop your presentation, you are also soft-marketing the upcoming series.

Rules of thumbs are seldom right for specific industries, but they are a good place to start. Many people recommend promoting your webinar event six weeks in advance. To some, this may seem too far in advance; however, in the corporate world, if we are promoting a big, mega webinar with a worldwide audience, we would start more than six weeks out. Don't forget that you need to get all the promotional materials prepared, prepare your list and make sure everyone involved is well aware of the event, especially if you have a big-name speaker.

When conducting webinars outside of a corporate role, we'd recommend conducting a major marketing effort at least four weeks in advance. The earlier you start the better. Six weeks sure sounds like a long time, but it goes quickly - and it allows enough time to get on people's schedules before they fill up.

Currently many of the popular information marketers are recommending 3 day or less for recruiting to webinars. This again comes down to knowing your audience.

Reminders Are a Great Form of Marketing

Promoting your event early is smart, because most of your prospects don't necessarily schedule much very far in advance. The downside is that people often forget events they've scheduled far in advance. Therefore, reminders of the event, *after* the sign-up, are a critically important part of the marketing process.

Here is an example list of emailed reminders that should be send following a webinar sign-up.

1. **Thank You for Signing-Up Email (Required)** Send immediately following the sign-up and include an "Add

to your Calendar" link so that recipients can easily put it on their schedule.

2. **Weekly / Bi-weekly Email (Optional)** Send an email message with a valuable tip or info once per week leading up to the webinar. Include a reminder of the upcoming webinar in your message. Make sure the content is valuable and relevant, so you don't run the risk of causing a qualified prospect to opt out prematurely.

3. **One Week Before the Event (Required)** Send a reminder of the event along with an "Add to your Calendar" link the week just prior to the webinar. You might also include a message asking recipients to share the message with their colleagues who might also be interested. The message should include a description of the event and that you expect a large number of people to attend, so you recommend they show up early.

4. **One Day Before (Required)** Send a reminder one day in advance of the webinar to keep it on their minds. This message should also include a "buzz-generating" statement about a large number of sign-ups, if appropriate.

5. **One Hour Before (Required)** Send an email message one hour before. This gives your attendees a chance to prepare for the webinar by clearing their computers, putting the phone on hold and removing distractions. In fact, this message should suggest exactly that. (Advanced Tip: Send a text reminder message too at this time.)

6. **Minutes Before the Start (Optional)** Send one more short and sweet email message simply stating that your webinar is starting now, and include a link to the webinar in the message. I can't tell you how many times this simple message has gotten Melodie and I to wrap up a phone call quickly so we could get into a webinar we might have forgotten about in the moment. (Advanced Tip: Send one more very short text letting them know the webinar has started.)

That's it. This routine will give people every opportunity to remember to attend your webinar. Unfortunately, you're human, and running a reminder program like this would probably be a very big burden if you were to do it manually. That's where automation comes to the rescue.

Melodie and Carl use an automated reminder and follow-up system. We schedule every one of these emails and text messages in advance. The system then sends them out according to the rules we specify, following a successful sign-up. If the prospective attendee provides their mobile number, the system will also send out the text messages. We also program the system to follow-up with people that attended the webinar with a "Thank you", a reminder of our offer or news of other upcoming webinars/events. Also, send a "Sorry we missed you" message with a link to the replay to those who signed up but did not attend.

Paid-For and Free Webinars

Many clients ask if they should be offering free webinars or if their attendees should pay to attend their webinars. The answer depends on the purpose of your webinar, the type of webinar you're offering and the target audience. It's certainly nice to get paid for our work, but there are a couple of reasons to do both free and paid webinars.

If you're looking to build your list and build authority in your marketplace, offering free webinars with valuable information is an effective strategy. Free webinars often see higher sign-up rates. However, it is critical that the webinar offers valuable information which attendees can use immediately, and isn't just a sales pitch for your products.

Paid webinars have a higher up-front perceived value, so you need to ensure that you deliver on that perception by the end of the webinars. Though it's often true that paid webinars have lower sign-up rates, they do tend to have a higher show-up rate. Additionally, the up-front payment (no matter how small or large) tends to qualify prospects that are truly interested in what you are offering. Online training and online education are good examples of successful paid webinars.

The Free-To-Fee model is an effective webinar strategy. In this strategy, you deliver a free webinar with solid valuable content, such as tips or how-tos; content that promises to make a real difference in the attendee's personal or professional life. This webinar is offered free, with the aim of getting them onto your marketing list, so that you can promote the next paid webinar event. This promises to take them to the next level, by expanding on the information you provided in the first free webinar. We suggest you call paid webinars online education, an online group coaching session or online training services.

Think of the free webinar as an initial consultation. It allows prospective customers to get to know, like and trust you, establishing your authority as an expert in your field. You want to lead them to either your consulting service or perhaps even automated or personal webinars that people would pay to participate in. Those would be very appropriate for business coaches and life coaches. It's a great methodology to get people moving toward your product or service.

Get The Ultimate Webinar Planning Checklist

To get the Ultimate Webinar Planning Checklist (includes step by step for before, during and after) go to
www.DeliverWebinars.com

Chapter Five

Making the Most of Your Webinar – Leverage

Let's discuss leverage. Leverage is the greatest feature of preparing and conducting webinars. In this chapter, we will only skim the surface of how to leverage your webinars into multiple formats of content, but we will definitely stimulate your thinking.

So, when it comes to a webinar, what is leverage? Well, from a single webinar you can produce several articles which you can post on your website, send to the local newspaper or post on LinkedIn. You can publish several informational videos on Youtube, with links back to your website. After you're done, you also have a rough draft for a pamphlet or book which you could publish on Amazon.com. Not to mention the countless topics and snippets you could create to post on social media networks... and the list goes on.

That's what this chapter is all about. Getting the most from your efforts to develop and present your webinar… or, simply put, maximizing your leverage!

First things first - recording

The first thing you need to do to leverage your webinar into other sources of content is to record it. That might seem obvious to many of you reading this book; however, many webinars are basically thought of as one-offs and don't get recorded. Our recommendation is to record every webinar you do, even the practice webinars; you never know what you might be able to use later.

One the one hand, recording can be quite easy; on the other hand, at times it's somewhat tricky. Many of the webinar services offer a recording feature, so it's just a matter of clicking a button or two and the recording starts. With Google Hangouts, when you hit the broadcast button it will go live in just a few seconds and be recorded automatically. GoToMeeting and GoToWebinar offer recording as a standard feature. If you have a webinar service that doesn't offer recording, you can use a recording software package like Camtasia or ScreenFlow. Sometimes, recording from the webinar services does not work and so additionally recording with Camtasia or ScreenFlow will give you a backup plan.

Our top tip to record your webinar - use the recording service if it's available. If not, use recording software. It's much better to use the recording service because it is being recorded at the source of the streaming, rather than capturing it on your own computer where the video quality is not going to be as good. The audio may not match up with the mouth movement, but it's a good backup to have just in case.

Remember that most of the services record in a proprietary file type that will need to be converted if you want to edit or share with others, so they can use standard video players. If necessary, hire a consultant to do the conversion and edit the video for you. With Google Hangouts, you can download in a common video file type, so it's easy to edit.

Next Step in Leveraging Your Webinar - Transcribing

The second critical step to leveraging your webinar is to get someone to transcribe the audio into a digital word-processing document. Though there is software available that will attempt to transcribe the audio, we highly recommend hiring a transcriber to take care of it for you.

Geek Tip: YouTube now has transcription software available for uploaded videos. However, we have seen mixed results with this service so we still recommend that you hire someone to transcribe the audio for you.

Now that you have a recording and a transcription, you can start leveraging your webinars.

Leveraging examples

Here are some examples of leveraging webinar content and video to help stimulate your creativity:

- **Offer On-Demand Viewing** Get your recording edited and offer the replay on your website. Make sure that you get "paid" for each person that wants to view it. By "paid," we don't necessarily always mean cash money. You could require people to sign up with their name and email address in order to view the replay... though getting paid money is nice, too.

- **Your Videos Are a Source of Articles** We haven't met many clients (with the exception of authors) who absolutely love to write articles. The most common complaint is, "I don't know what to write about." Webinars offer an almost automatic source of article ideas and content. In our experience, one recorded video presentation can be leveraged into at least two or three articles. A benefit of live presentations is that you will naturally convey your knowledge about your subject matter. When speaking, you're likely to present that knowledge in a way that is more understandable to your audience than you would if you started out by writing it all down. By recording and transcribing your presentations, you can become a regular article writer in due time.

- **Podcasting** An obvious part of a video is the audio track. Leverage this audio into a podcast that you can post in the iTunes, Stitcher or Google play or other podcast directories. With podcasting, you can offer your target market a free or paid subscription to your audio content; and with a little extra work on your part (or a consultant's part), you can leverage all your videos into traffic. You should also note that podcasting is not just limited to audio (mp3); you can also post the entire video as a podcast too (mp4).

- **Create a Course** As you create and record your webinars, you will most likely find that they have a common theme throughout (or perhaps you can create them according to a common theme by design). Why not bundle the videos together and market them as a complete course? Create a membership-based website, to which people can subscribe, in order to get access to all your previously recorded webinars. Membership could be a paid service, or you could use it to build your list. Either way, this is a good way to get much more value out of your previous work effort.

- **E-Book - Think Kindle** Developing, conducting and recording webinars is a great way to write a book. Just like article writing, you will have the webinar recording transcribed; and this transcription makes a great first rough draft of a book. Polish that rough draft into a book yourself (or hire a consultant to help you through it) and now you can publish your book on the world's largest bookstore, Amazon.com. Plus, as a bonus, Amazon will let you create an author page on their website to help you get even more traffic and credibility. And as a bonus you can then turn your e-book into a physical book using Createspace and offer it on Amazon.com as well.

- **Social Media** Everyone and just about every business on the planet seems to have a Facebook page. It's not hard to get into social media; the tough part is keeping up with it. Success with social media requires activity - and activity means publishing content. Remember our comment above that most people don't like to write and seem to not be able to determine what to write about - that's where your webinar comes into play. After transcribing your webinar, you should highlight all the concepts you addressed. Then, sit down for just one hour and write short paragraph posts about each of those concepts. When you're done, we bet that you'll have at least a week or two's worth of social media posts ready to go. Schedule them to be posted live over the next couple of weeks and you'll soon be knows as a social media guru.

- **Video Casting** Sure, you can post your entire recorded webinar for replay; however, you could also break it up into concepts and post several traffic-attracting videos from the same webinar. Create an intro and outro that you can reuse on each of the videos; the former should introduce the concept covered, while the latter should then direct the viewer to your website where they can get even more information. Use video editing software to cut each concept into one- to three-minute video clips you can use. A one-hour webinar recording could easily be leveraged into anything from three to ten quality, three-minute concept videos, which you can post on YouTube, LinkedIn and social media sites.

It's all about leverage. Before you even start designing your next webinar, write down all the ways that you can use the recorded content. Create a schedule for when and how you will use it and get the most from your creative effort.

Get A List Of Recommended Resources

To get a list of recommended resources (updated often with any new services) go to **www.DeliverWebinars.com**

Chapter Six

Tips for Creating the Best Webinar Possible

Here are some tips we've put together from our many years of experience creating, delivering and attending webinars. It's much better to learn from the mistakes of others (in this case, us) rather than head down that trail for the first time yourself. The majority of these tips come from our doing the exact opposite on a past occasion; after all, experience is often the best teacher.

Don't Underestimate the Importance of Audio Quality

After valuable content, the next critical concern should be great audio. If your audio quality is good, people will forgive just about anything else that might be off about your presentation. Be sure your audio stream is working well and that your audience can hear and understand you clearly. Enlist the help of an assistant. We usually call that position a producer or a facilitator. This is someone who can help you with the behind-the-scenes tasks and logistics and monitor the chat log for you. The producer can help with technical issues, can be the host or emcee and can let you know if there's a problem. When you're presenting, you may not realize that your audio or your video has gone down. The producer can monitor this.

Speak clearly and loudly and take the time to breathe. Those are the three keys to really good audio. Show your passion and your enthusiasm for the subject. If you're presenting, hopefully you care about the subject and that will translate to the audience. You should keep the mindset that you are performing the webinar, since a performance mentality will help you to breathe life into your presentation, rather than just deliver it. Don't be that monotonous, boring science teacher you had in high school; perform and people will engage.

Using and Handling Visuals

Create compelling content with compelling visuals. Slides are a great visual. If you're going to use videos, test them out first. Some of the services play videos really well and some don't; so be sure you know what your audience is seeing. Prepare the video ahead of time, by either creating a short clip of the information you want to present from the video, or by making a note of the start and end time of the portion of the video. No one wants to show up at a webinar to watch a video - unless, of course, the video is you performing your webinar.

Practice, practice, practice

Practice, practice, practice. Practice your presentation, practice using the software, practice using all of the tools you plan on using. Don't overlook the power of practice; practice will help you perform your webinar rather than read it. Practice will also give you more confidence with your content, the technology and presenting online. You won't regret practice - trust us on this.

Be Early – Test Early – Start on Time

Start on time; this is another key point. I've been on webinars where the presenters show up five minutes late - that's just not showing respect to the people who are there on time. It is a best practice to be online a minimum of 15 minutes early and ready to go; be 30 minutes early if there are many attendees. Being early gives you a chance to test the service by doing a sound check, checking that your visuals show up and starting the recording. Don't start early, but definitely start on time.

> "I am usually on the webinar 30 minutes early, even if I am the only person. I go through my checklist. I don't like to rush. I want to check to ensure that everything is set

and ready to go by the time people appear. Sometimes, participants will appear 15 minutes early, and that gives me a chance to ask them why they're there and what they hope to learn. Then I can make sure that I cover those things for them. In short it's an additional chance for me to connect with my audience and build a relationship with them"
– Melodie Rush

Encourage your attendees to log on early, because sometimes they will have issues; for example, some of the webinar services require that you download a little piece of software before you can get on. First-time users will need to get on a couple of minutes early to make sure they have everything configured. A great way to get people to act quickly is to let them know attendance is limited during your promotional period.

Be organized

Be professional. Be organized. Make sure that the computer you are presenting from does not have a bunch of programs open. Turn off your Skype account, chat account, email notifications, etc. If you're using a slideshow program like PowerPoint® or Keynote®, have that open, your web browser open and your recording software open. Close down everything else.

Turn off all the other sounds, including your cell phone. Yes, make sure you turn the cell phone off (unless you're using it for the audio portion). Vibration is equally distracting. Turn off anything that makes noise. You want to ensure your audience that they are the focus of your attention and that you take what you are doing seriously.

Leave time at the end for questions and answers; this allows you to interact with your audience and that's what they're looking for. It helps you to establish trust and build a relationship with them.

Use a checklist; keep a running checklist that you can update as you make mistakes or recognize an opportunity. This checklist will be invaluable to you for each and every future webinar you present.

Have a backup plan. Bring your cell phone. Sometimes my audio doesn't work on my Voice over IP phones, so I have my cellphone available (and charged). Have a printed copy of your slides: let's say your computer dies or your internet quits. If you have an assistant or are using a producer at a remote location, you can dial in on your telephone, refer to your printed slides and the producer can change the slides as you speak.

There will be issues; just be ready to work through them calmly. People understand, so just be ready. The more webinars you do, the more technical issues you're going to understand; and the more you're going to be prepared and the more comprehensive and valuable your checklist will be.

Just be yourself and you won't look like an idiot. People will get to know you and that's what you really want to happen.

Treat this webinar as if you're going to meet with these 100 people personally. Dress appropriately; be respectful; but also, show some passion. Don't drone on and on in a dull voice. You'll make mistakes, but everybody makes a few mistakes. If you practice, they'll be minimal.

The Challenge of Technology

What technology gives, it often takes away. Technology can be the biggest challenge. Today's webinar services are much better than they used to be; in the early days there were lots of technical problems. There are still some technical problems today and frankly, sometimes things just don't work. You need a backup plan to make sure that you can do what you need to do - we usually have a plan B, C and D when we do webinars. For example, we do a lot webinars where we use telephones for the audio part and we always have my cellphone available, because once in a while, Voice over IP phones just don't work. We can't fix that. It's just the way the service is sometimes.

Here is a funny story that occurred during an online education program that we were facilitating. We tell our clients that there's almost nothing we can do if the internet goes down; however, we also tell them that we will do everything in our power to try to get something together. These students are paying quite a bit of money and if they miss a night, it's difficult for the instructors to make that up. In the last four years, I think we've only missed two nights due to a major power outage.

Anyway, back to the story. One night, the instructor was not able to broadcast audio over his computer. The slides were working, everything was working, but the audio was just not streaming. It was just all broken up and students were complaining. I did everything I could from where I was, but the instructor's internet connection was no good and the service we were using did not have a phone bridge. I only had a few minutes to come up with a solution before the students would start giving up - so I pulled a MacGyver.

I had the instructor call me via my landline telephone and I duct-taped the telephone to my computer's microphone. We broadcast audio for the next two and half hours, just like that. The instructor didn't even know what I had done until we met at a Veterinary conference a couple of months later! Sometimes you just have to go old school.

Make sure your hardware and software is in good working order. If you have a wireless mouse, check your batteries. If you have an ethernet network wired to your internet router, use it rather than Wi-Fi. The better the internet, the better your overall presentation is going to be.

Technical challenges are a given. The more options you have to handle the challenges, the better the webinar will be.

Choosing a Topic

A webinar is a flexible format which accommodates just about any topic. Our best advice is to go in-depth into a narrow topic rather than to skim the surface on a broad topic. Be clear to your audience what you will be presenting and make sure you present what you say you will.

Knowing your audience will allow you to know if you need to spend more time going over basics, or if going deeper will be a better option. A good rule of thumb is to stick to two or three key points for 30 minutes of content, or four or five key points for 60 minutes of content.

Taking Questions during a Webinar

You absolutely should take questions during a webinar. However, if you're new to performing webinars and are trying to juggle all of these things yourself answering questions may throw you off your flow. Starting out, we recommend that you hold questions to the end. Just ask them to type their questions in the chat window and let them know you will address them at the end. That way, people can feel engaged and know that questions will be answered later - but it won't break up your flow.

Once you get more experience, you may want to take questions during your presentation. Stop at certain breakpoints and take questions. You can also ask your attendees questions that they can answer in the chat window; this will keep attendees more engaged and involved in your presentation.

We often take questions throughout our webinars. With a large audience, we only take questions via Chat. If it is a smaller audience, then we allow questions live, via the phone or computer audio connection. Many times questions can be a distraction and throw you off course. However, taking questions and answering them throughout your presentation keeps the audience more engaged. That's the trade-off.

If you're going to take questions throughout your webinar, it really helps to have a producer or facilitator who can pick out questions, which are appropriate to what you're talking about. This prevents you from going off on a tangent and having to struggle back on path to your original planned content.

Consider Using a Producer

There are five roles producers or facilitators can fill for a webinar:

1. Host, emcee or interviewer
2. Interaction support
3. Question minder
4. Technical support
5. Coach

Host, emcee, or interviewer. This makes for a very dynamic presentation because it gives you a chance to think; and often, a professional producer can help emphasize key points.

Interaction support. Sometimes, you might get questions in the Q&A window that your producer can answer himself or herself without interrupting you, or that you won't need to answer. As you do more and more webinars, you'll see that there's a common set of questions which get asked, but which don't necessarily have to be addressed as part of the webinar. A producer can answer these through the Q&A window using a FAQ sheet you provide ahead of time.

Question minder. A producer can monitor the chat window for questions from participants. Determine up front with your producer when and how to interrupt you during the presentation to answer a question. Often a producer may recognize a question that is appropriate at that time and will add value to the webinar. Otherwise, the producer can make a log of questions to ask you at the end, in an interview style.

Technical support. A professional producer often provides technical support to both you and your audience. By monitoring the webinar from the audience's side, a producer can let you know the status of your audio or video stream. A specific number of attendees will inevitably have some sort of trouble, and a producer can handle those issues for you so it won't interrupt your presentation or the other audience members who are not experiencing any difficulty. If there are glitches, a producer can alert you and help you to troubleshoot them. They can also help you to set up the session, get you started, mute lines and be your time keeper if some people will have to be reminded. They can inform presenters that there's 10 minutes left or there's 5 minutes left, or whatever.

A Coach. A professional producer is your coach. They help you avoid some of those pitfalls and common mistakes that everyone makes; you can learn from their experience. Producers can also introduce your session and teach the attendees how to participate, by sharing housekeeping things, such as how and when to ask questions. If you have a session where people are on the phone, a producer can ask them to mute their lines. A producer can also handle the polls for you and cue interactive things, which occur in the webinar. A producer makes you look very professional, kind of like Ed McMahon introducing Johnny Carson on *The Tonight Show*.

Importantly, a producer makes sure that the recording gets started. Don't ask us how many times we forgot to do that for ourselves; too many to count!

Having a producer takes away some of that anxiety which naturally occurs as we get started doing webinars and takes some of the pressure off the presenter. We have facilitated many webinars for clients creating online training, sales presentations and software demos. It's very helpful to have a producer, whether you're a beginner or an experienced webinar presenter.

Teach Your Attendees How to Participate

It probably sounds funny to say, "Teach people how to listen to you," but it is an important point - especially when it comes to webinars. Unlike in-person seminars, you can not see the individuals in the audience of a webinar. There is nothing stopping them from being distracted or not paying attention.

Encourage them to turn off all the applications and gizmos, which might distract them. I think it's fine to ask your attendees this by saying, "You know I've got an hour's worth of content here. It's going to be well worth your time; so I just ask you to turn off the cell phone and turn off other applications on your computer and just give me an hour's worth of your time. It will be well worth it." I think that sometimes, just letting people know that makes them think, "Oh man, I just got caught." You're simply reminding them to be self-disciplined.

Content is king; so make sure you have compelling content. If you're using slides, make sure that they're easy to read and easy to follow. I see a lot of people using slides and you can't read them because the font is too small. Think about it: sometimes people are going to be on their cell phone watching your webinar, so if you've have lots of text on the slide they're not going to be able to see it and you're going to lose their attention.

If you use slides, it's okay to use some animation - but don't go crazy. Some animation will keep people interested, but too much of it might not show up; that's one thing to practice too. I've seen some animation that just won't work across the network, so keep it simple if you're going to use it.

Have a Quiet Place

Sure, this might seem obvious, but are you sure the place you have in mind is truly quiet? You need to have a quiet place without disruption. We talked about turning off everything, but also consider kids, spouses or co-workers that might unwittingly (or wittingly) interrupt you. Put a little hangtag outside the door or a sign that reads: "Quiet - webinar in progress." This will keep people from busting in on you or knocking on your door.

You should also run a quick test recording of the room. Set up a webinar and hit the record button. Do a quick: "Testing one-two-three," and then let the webinar software record the quiet room. Listen to the recording for that background noise that you've been ignoring for years, such as a fan, noisy equipment, gurgling aquarium, etc. Eliminate the source if you can.

We've said it before, we'll say it again: audio, audio, audio. Your audience needs to be able to hear you loud and clear; even if they can't see, they need to hear. This is absolutely critical to a successful webinar.

Are they sleeping? – getting your audience engaged

We've talked about good content and the need to perform your webinars with passion in order to get people engaged. It's important to recognize that your audience is easily distracted by email, Skype, internet browsing and other multi-tasking temptations. Here are some ideas on how to keep their attention:

- Ask questions of the audience during the webinar, and acknowledge people by name when they answer. People love to hear their names. Asking questions will also let you measure the engagement. Ask them questions and they can respond in the chat window. You can say "How many of you have done *x*?" or "How many of you are interested in this?" and you can see if people are responding to your questions. This will tell you if they're engaged.

- Using some of those other tools we've talked about, like polls, can help.
- I've seen people use giveaways or prizes, typically at the end (and actually even in the middle), and that also keeps people engaged. If they think they can win something, they will keep listening.

Some of the services have tools which show you how engaged your audience is. You'll be able to see how many people have logged in and how many people are logging out during the course of your webinar. Some services will even show you whether or not that person is focused on the window where your webinar is being shown, or whether they're off surfing on another window.

It will show you that they're there but not focused in on that particular tool, so you can get a feel for that.

One other tip: if you are going to do a webinar, make sure that you're not broadcasting how many viewers you have on the webinar - unless you know you're going to have a ton. If you've got this incredible list and you know for sure you're going to have 300 to 400 people, then I would recommend that you have a Facebook streaming chat or some sort of streaming chat in there so that the audience can see each other and talk to each other (if they choose to do so).

However, I wouldn't recommend you do that unless you know you're going to have a lot of people. There's nothing worse than trying to get a lot of energy out there with the webinar when it's showing there are only five people on the webinar at any given moment - and everybody else knows it. It's kind of a downer.

What's in the Background?

If you're doing a live video feed, keep your background simple and uncluttered. The background should only contain items you want the audience to see. Keep it simple! Simplicity will keep people more focused on you and not on what's going on in the background. We've seen some funny backgrounds, where objects made it look like the presenters had horns growing out of the back of their heads. It was funny - but it was distracting.

Take a close look at anything hanging on the walls. Melodie once attended a webinar with a very "manly man" speaking and the picture above his office desk was a huge picture of kittens. It was distracting and didn't match him or the image he was trying to project. (That's not to say that "manly men" can't like kittens, but it might be good to take a look at the background and determine if it is the image you want to project.)

Deliver Webinars Like A Pro

If you have a lot of clutter in the background, put a screen up behind you. Pick a nice color for the screen, though a plain white background always works.

If you're going to do screen sharing, you want to make sure that your computer desktop is clean, so that people don't see distracting things on your computer screen. Get rid of extra icons and anything else, which is not part of the webinar. Today, this is easy; just make a folder with a simple name and drag all of the icons into it. Then, after the webinar, you can drag them all out again, if you like.

Only open the applications, which you need for the webinar. It's nice to have a second screen where you can hide a lot of material that you're using for your presentation, like the controls to the webinar. I think whether you're doing a live feed or you're talking about screen sharing, just keep it simple and uncluttered and you'll be in good shape.

Lighting on the Set

Lighting is only important if you're on a live video webcam. If you're not doing a live video stream, you can do it in the dark if you want to. If you're in front of the camera, you need to have very good light and you want to have light in front of you. I've seen many, many webinars where people are just dimly lit and you can't see them. In fact they look like they are in witness protection. Probably not the image they want to project unless of course they are in witness protection. If you can't see them, there's no need of doing a live feed. You might as well just stick with slides.

Lighting a webinar is very much like lighting for a video shoot. Use a simple three-point lighting system if possible. It all depends on the webcam you're using; a lot of webcams will accommodate for lighting. We recommend that you go shopping and get a few of them, try them all out and then choose the best one. You can return the others. We usually use the room light and natural light from the window. You don't want to have a really bright light behind you. For example, if the sun is glaring through a window behind you, it's going to silhouette you and make you darker; so just use typical video lighting guidelines and you'll be fine. Use an assistant or producer to check your video stream for lighting issues.

If your audio is good, people will forgive some of the video - and you don't always have to be in the video. A lot of the webinars I see are simply slides or on-screen software demonstrations.

Another video tip is to keep the webcam at eye level or slightly above eye level. This will compliment your face; not to mention the fact that videos looking up people's noses can be quite distracting.

Join Our Facebook Group

Go to www.DeliverWebinars.com

Next Steps

Time to get started. Take all the lessons learned in this book and complete your first webinar. For additional help check out the resources below.

If you have additional questions, please contact us. We look forward to not only answering your questions but also hearing about your successes with webinars.

- **Connect with Melodie at**
  - Website www.melodierush.com
  - FaceBook - www.facebook.com/wecreatemvps
  - Twitter https://twitter.com/WeCreateMVPs
  - LinkedIn - https://www.linkedin.com/in/melodierush
  - GooglePlus - https://plus.google.com/+MelodieRush1

- ○ **Connect with Carl at**
  - ▪ Website www.civicmindmedia.com
  - ▪ FaceBook - www.facebook.com/carlstearns
  - ▪ Twitter https://twitter.com/carlstearns
  - ▪ LinkedIn -
    https://www.linkedin.com/in/civicmindmedia/
  - ▪ GooglePlus - https://plus.google.com/+CarlStearns-Marketing-Consultant

To get a copy of the Ultimate Checklist for Delivering a Webinar like a Pro go to www.DeliverWebinars.com.

Join our Facebook group by visiting www.DeliverWebinars.com

Please subscribe to the podcast "The Webinar Report" on iTunes, Stitcher, or Google Play

For additional marketing information get a copy of our mastermind book "There's Money in this Book" on Amazon.com.

For additional one-on-one help we offer 4 options:

- **Self paced online training and membership site** http://www.webinarmasterb2p.com/web_product
- **Coaching Program** Five 30-minute sessions
  - What to do before
  - What to do during
  - What to do after
  - Creating Slides/Handouts
  - Ninja tricks (planning for success)
- **Professional Webinar Producer**
  - Set-up Session
  - Practice Session
  - Live Session
  - Record
  - Manage Q&A
- **Webinar tune-up**
  - Listen to and provide feedback on any webinar
  - Feedback includes what you did well and what can be improved

Additional Resources

To get a list of resources, join our Facebook Group, and get updates to this book go to
www.DeliverWebinars.com

Please contact us with questions or for more information.

56492200R10045

Made in the USA
Charleston, SC
21 May 2016